Writing in an Era of Conflict

Richard Rhodes
and
Thomas L. Friedman

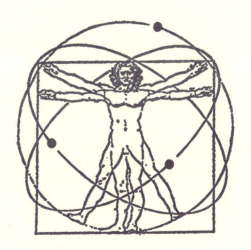

Library of Congress
Washington
1990

The publication of this book was made possible through private contributions to the Center for the Book and the National Book Foundation.

The Center for the Book is also grateful to the Verner W. Clapp Publications Fund for its support.

Library of Congress Cataloging-in-Publication Data

Rhodes, Richard.
   Writing in an era of conflict / Richard Rhodes and Thomas L. Friedman.
      p. cm. — (The National book week lectures)
   Includes bibliographical references.
   Contents: The flesh made word / Richard Rhodes — The writing life / Thomas L. Friedman.
   ISBN 0-8444-0709-7 (alk. paper)
—— —— Copy 3 Z663.118 .W73 1990
   1. Books and reading. 2. Authorship. I. Friedman, Thomas L.
II. Title. III. Series.
Z1003.R45 1990
808'.02—dc20   90-22825
                                  CIP

The paper in the publication meets the requirements for permanence established by the American National Standard for Information Science "Permanence of Paper for Printed Library Materials," ANSI Z39-48-1984.

CONTENTS

PREFACE

These two lectures, presented at the Library of Congress by National Book Award winners Richard Rhodes and Thomas L. Friedman, inaugurate both a new published lecture series and a new partnership. The partners are the Center for the Book in the Library of Congress and the National Book Foundation, which sponsors the National Book Awards. This joint venture springs from a common goal: the desire to stimulate public awareness and appreciation of books, writers, and the values of a literate and creative society. National Book Week, celebrated the fourth week of each January, is a week-long celebration of American books and writers which features writers talking about their writing. The Center for the Book and the National Book Foundation invite libraries, schools, universities, and other groups to mark National Book Week 1991 (January 20–26) by inviting a local writer to discuss what it means to be a writer.

Richard Rhodes won the National Book Award in 1987 for his book *The Making of the Atomic Bomb* (Simon & Schuster, 1986). The same work won the National Book Critics Circle Award in 1987 and the Pulitzer Prize in 1988. Since then Mr. Rhodes has published *Farm* (Simon & Schuster, 1989) and *A Hole in the World: An American Boyhood* (Simon & Schuster, 1990). His lecture was presented at the Library of Congress on November 28, 1988.

Thomas L. Friedman won the National Book Award in 1989 for his book *From Beirut to Jerusalem* (Farrar, Straus and Giroux, 1989). The chief diplomatic correspondent of the *New York Times*, Friedman is a two-time winner of the Pulitzer Prize (1983 and 1988) for his reporting from the Middle East. His National Book Week lecture was presented at the Library of Congress on January 23, 1990.

The Center for the Book in the Library of Congress was established in 1977 to stimulate public interest in books, reading, and libraries and to encourage the study of books. The projects of the Center for the Book and its twenty-three state affiliates are supported by tax-deductible contributions from individuals and corporations.

John Y. Cole
Director
The Center for the Book

INTRODUCTION

The mission of The National Book Foundation is to raise the cultural value of good writing in America. We aim to accomplish this in two broad areas.

Currently, we are commemorating the fortieth anniversary of the National Book Awards. Their prestige remains inestimable, and their cachet pervasive. The foundation board and staff are committed to enhancing the quality of the awards, as a tribute to all writers.

Through a newly developed community program in collaboration with the Center for the Book in the Library of Congress, we present National Book Award winners and nominees in settings around the country, talking about their craft—"The Writing Life"—and their motivations—"The Pleasures of Reading." We intend to enlist the energies of our great authors, to part the veil slightly before the literary work, and to share some of its miraculous secrets with ever-broader audiences.

Thus, it is a pleasure to introduce these essays by the 1987 and 1989 National Book Award winners for nonfiction, the first volume in a series to be copublished with our institutional partner, the Center for the Book in the Library of Congress.

Richard Rhodes presents a spiritual and poetic hymn of praise to the body as the source of all good and a warning to mankind that the roots for ultimate destruction likewise reside within the body.

The theme is appropriate for the author of *The Making of the Atomic Bomb*. In these parlous times, Rhodes issues a clarion call for imaginative self-knowledge as the basis for human salvation. The perils of technological advancement coexisting with its benefits provide the tense subtext for Rhodes's essay, at once cautionary and speculative. The ultimate (ironic) achievement is splitting the atom, source of unparalleled energy as well as the death-machine seedbed for nuclear winter.

Rhodes meditatively pivots his essay upon the many paradoxes embodied in postmodern life. At last, he opts for the life of the mind manifested in art, the fruits of the creative act and the imagination, especially the word, logos, as mankind's great and saving grace.

Thomas Friedman's lecture, delivered during National Book Week in January 1990 at the Library of Congress, may be read as a vibrant exemplar of Rhodes's final thesis, a fanciful, supremely entertaining reply, grounded in the reality of journalism at its most highly developed. It is the impassioned journalism of a man who has "been there," and who has borne witness to the most extreme human conflict of our era.

Friedman thrives upon immediacy. Indeed, what has made his brand of journalism so special is his uncanny ability to live inside the reality he is then able to write about through force of will, shaping a kind of charged objectivity—anecdotes layered so thickly the reader can feel the texture of lived situations through political complexity and quotidian life fragmented by violence.

Thomas Friedman's remarks on the writing life from Beirut to Jerusalem to Washington are by an admittedly obsessed student of reality, presented in a conversational tone which belies their deeply serious intent: to probe the nature of a genre meant to tell the firm truth in a shifting world.

Neil Baldwin
Executive Director
The National Book Foundation

THE FLESH MADE WORD

In the beginning was the Word.

For the divine it may have been,
but not for man and woman. In the beginning for man and woman
was the flesh, the body, the poor, bare, forked animal, the thing itself.
In the end for man and woman shall be the body as well, crushed or
perhaps resplendent. We are born and bathed in body, we live in body,
in body we die.

Anatomy is destiny. Body is all we were given, all we have, all we
ever know. The surface of our skin is the map and history of the world:
peaks of reason, valleys of flesh, between them mute tectonic relations.
The miraculous web of nerves that sensitizes the body's surface, the
voiceless projections with which it explores, the velvet membranes that
warm and lubricate its openings propose a bodily relation to the world.

But flesh is pain, inarticulate body is pain, silence and incapacity
are pain. Not to know, not to have words to speak, is to suffer. "Nature
is a tropical swamp in sunshine," says Emerson, "on whose purlieus we
hear the song of summer birds, and see prismatic dewdrops—but her
interiors are terrific, full of hydras and crocodiles."

The slow unfolding of the body from its primordial silence has
been the work of imagination since the beginning of human time, the
great human project. In tools and language first of all, in elaborations
next of agriculture and of religion, now increasingly in science, and

1

always along the way in the sturdy alleviations of craft and vernacular technology, our species extends its collective body into the world. Our eyes elongated into spacecraft explore the surface of Mars. Our hands enlarged into cranes and mills and refineries transform Emerson's terrific interiors into instruments and engines of process, into structures of shelter and peaceful gardens. Electronic networks accelerate our thoughts, networks of light communicate our speech, menacing networks of missiles picket our fears. "It is part of the work of creating," writes the critic Elaine Scarry, "to deprive the external world of the privilege of being inanimate."[1] Depriving the external world of the privilege of being inanimate is just the work of these bodies, of these eyes and hands and mouths, of these instruments of sound and light and connection, of these brushes and wheels, of this paper and this pen, of these books. Blind oracles have done it and saviors, grimy miners digging ore, scholars parsing texts, natural philosophers winding magnets, seamstresses sewing clothes, revolutionaries composing declarations of truths never before self-evident. Roof tiles and suture needles, cheese and tatami mats and the abolition of slavery are acts of creation. Hybrid corn is a gift of life.

"We can know more than we can tell," writes the philosopher of science Michael Polanyi.[2] Whenever we know what we mean to say before we say it, we know more than we can tell. Whenever we feel the implicit meanings of situations, and experience those situations not as facts to be examined but as moments to be lived, we know more than we can tell. Whenever we accept the truth of a discovery, freighted as all true discoveries are with undisclosed and perhaps yet unthinkable consequences, we know more than we can tell.[3]

We can know more than we can tell because the body is the ground and only vessel of experience. It extends itself into the world by imitation and analogy. The hand grasping an object, the eye and ear and nose and tongue grasping an object make a negative of the object, an imitation, a mold. The molds are stored in memory and accumulate. Eventually they assemble an image even in the object's absence. The image replaces the absent object and constructs continuity. Thus the body modifies the world and captures it, making it available for thought, for language, and for alteration.[4]

The oldest words we know, the old Indo-European roots, were concrete and bodily. Analogy—metaphor—elaborated them, one end anchored still in body, the other end a fishing rod cast out into the world. Indo-European *ker*—heat, fire—from whence carbon and cremate and ceramic. Indo-European *kelp*—to hold, to grasp—from whence helm and halberd and halter. *Djku,* sweet; *dub*, to drop; *drem,* to sleep; *el,* red; *esen,* harvest; *er,* earth; *ere,* to row. *Ghei*—to yawn— from whence yawn and chasm and gasp and gill. *Angh*—tight, pain- fully constricted—from whence nail, anger, anguish, angina. *Sta[h]*— to stand, that which stands—from whence this bounty: steed and stud, stool, stow, stage, stanza, statue, arrest, circumstance, contrast, cost, distant, oust, obstacle, substitute, superstition, standard, armistice, starling and state, statistics and starboard and steer, store and restore, assist and consist and exist and persist, apostasy and epistemology and prostate and stoic and post.

From simple to complex, growth and elaboration, and sometimes back to simple again. Physics came to a day when bombarding a solution of uranium nitrate with neutrons resulted in the creation of barium, element 56, only about half as heavy as element 92. What was barium doing in that beaker where only uranium had been before? No one had imagined it, no one at first believed it, but there it was, and enormous binding energy released in the transformation, two hundred million electron volts when the most powerful atom smasher of the day could generate two or three million, energy sufficient from each individual fissioning uranium nucleus to make a visible grain of sand visibly jump. And instantly a few saw the possibility of a weapon of vast destruction, and not long afterward, a few saw that such a weapon could end a bloody war, and soon thereafter, a few saw that the threat of many such weapons would spoil world war and change the relations between the nation-states forever, change inexorably and without appeal to any higher power the dominant political system of the world, by forcing its modification away from belligerence or else blasting and burning it down. Because neutrons split heavy elements and release a squirt of heat besides. "When originality breeds new values," writes Michael Polanyi, "it breeds them tacitly, by implication; we cannot choose explicitly a set of new values, but must submit to them by the very act of creating or adopting them."[5] "If you are a scientist," Robert Oppenheimer told his crew of young weaponeers at Los Alamos in 1945 in the aftermath of Hiroshima and Nagasaki, "you believe that it is good to find out how the world works; that it is good to find out what the realities are; that it is good to turn over to mankind at large the greatest possible power to control the world and to deal with it according to its lights and it values . . . . It is not possible to be a scientist unless you believe that the knowledge of the world, and the power which this gives, is a thing which is of intrinsic value to humanity, and that you are using it to help in the spread of knowledge, and are willing to take the consequences."[6]

All this the body has done, to escape its painful silence. We are the beneficiaries of the human project, recipients made wealthy by its gifts. Therefore we owe it respect. But we owe it respect on its own terms. We owe it not uncritical affirmation. We owe it the effort to understand where it has worked and where it has failed. Only by studying its successes and mistakes, taking its measure, further enlarging its compass can we contribute to the ongoing project ourselves and prevent its foreclosure. "The imagination is not," Elaine Scarry asserts, "as has often been wrongly suggested, amoral: though she is certainly indifferent to many subjects that have in one era or another been designated 'moral,' the realm of her labor is centrally bound up with the elementary moral distinction between hurting and not hurting; she is simply, centrally, and indefatigably at work on behalf of sentience, eliminating its adversiveness and extending its acuity in forms as abundant, extravagantly variable, and startlingly unexpected as her ethical strictness is monotonous and narrowly consistent. The work of the imagination also overlaps with another interior human event that is usually articulated in a separate vocabulary, . . . for she is mixed up with (is in fact almost indistinguishable from) the phenomenon of compassion."[7] Neils Bohr identified a similar program for that kind of imagination which we call science: the goal of science, Bohr proposed, was not power over nature or an exact description of the world but "the gradual removal of prejudices."[8]

If meaning comes out of the body, the body is necessarily the final arbiter of meaning. When meaning is uncertain, when belief is in doubt, the body itself ultimately serves for authentication—by analogy where possible, by suffering where unavoidable, by wounding, as in torture and war, when less drastic methods fail. The body politic, we say, drawing the analogy, the head of state, the long arm of the law, but if you would join the group you must endure the initiation; if you would achieve the shrine you must struggle up the mountain; if you have shamed the Emperor you must commit ritual seppuku. The deepest discoveries in science and in art require at least provisional belief in the underlying order of the world even when only randomness is immediately evident. The cognitive and emotional dissonance such belief evokes is indistinguishable, until it resolves itself, from paranoia, and correspondingly painful.

Ultimately, when all else fails, we turn to wounding for authentication. "The dispute that leads to war," writes Elaine Scarry, "involves a process by which each side calls into question the legitimacy and thereby erodes the reality of the other country's issues, beliefs, ideas, self-conception. Dispute leads relentlessly to war not only because war is an extension and intensification of dispute but because it is a correction and reversal of it. That is, the injuring not only provides a means of choosing between disputants but also provides, by its massive opening of human bodies, a way of reconnecting the derealized and disembodied beliefs with the force and power of the material world."[9]

No wonder, then, that we scarify onto the bodies of those who differ from us the visible stigmata of their crimes. To despise another human being, to wound another human being, to open another human being's body in the name of proving a belief, requires denying those other human beings' essential humanity. Otherwise the wellsprings of compassion, of our profound and bodily identification with one another—all mothers, all fathers, all brothers and sisters and daughters and sons, all lovers and neighbors and friends—would flood the mechanism of alienation that cleaves us apart. We distance those whom we fear, and we fear them more for their distance. We distance them psychologically by reducing them to epithets: Hun, kike, Jap, kulak, gook, nigger, fascist, liberal, communist, Sandinista, enemy of the people, queer. We distance them physically by refusing to acknowledge their common humanity or to attend their suffering. Only then can we bear to injure or destroy them.

Technology amplifies this effect. Destruction at a distance with projectiles and bombs short-circuits the identification with similarly embodied beings, perhaps even the mammalian reflex,[10] that might otherwise stay our hand. More of this destruction, more man-made death, has occurred in the twentieth century than in any other century in the history of the world. "What will people of the future think of us?" asks C. P. Snow. "Will they say, as Roger Williams said of some of the Massachusetts Indians, that we were wolves with the minds of men? Will they think that we resigned our humanity? They will have the right."[11]

Ten million deaths, civilian and military, in the First World War. Fifteen million deaths in the Russian Civil War and another 20 million in Stalin's Great Terror. Twenty million Soviet civilian and combat deaths in the Second World War, 15 million deaths in Europe and Asia, 6 million European Jews murdered in the name of racial purity for a total of 41 million dead in the "good" war. Twenty million dead in China in the twentieth century from politically sponsored policies of famine, privation, and scorched earth. In gruesome total, more than 100 million man-made deaths up to the fifteenth of August 1945.[12] Since that August hinge, the number of wars has increased even as their death tolls have dramatically declined, but as of the end of 1987 there were twenty-two wars under way in the world, their deaths up to that date accumulating to some 2.2 million.[13]

Death tolls have declined, but the potential for man-made death is larger now by orders of magnitude than ever before. The Second World War consumed about five megatons of conventional explosives. Explosive equivalence of strategic weapons alone in the United States and the Soviet Union at the end of 1987 totaled nearly ten thousand megatons.[14] In 1984, the World Health Organization estimated that a ten-thousand megaton nuclear exchange would account for 1,150,000,000 deaths and 1,100,000,000 injuries.[15] It did not take fully into account the probability of a nuclear winter[16] and of AIDS-like mass immunodeficiency[17] as worldwide and devastating delayed effects. Despite those limitations, with subsequent deaths among the injured and mass starvation, the World Health Organization projected mortality approaches half the population of the earth. "The scale of man-made death," asserts the Scottish writer Gil Elliot, "is the central moral as well as material fact of our time."[18]

All these deaths, accomplished and potential, must weigh on our imagination, not to say our souls. Restraining them is the foremost assignment on the imagination's long, unfinished agenda. Since 1945 that agenda has no longer been open-ended. Brooding over its progress, a sphinx or a minotaur, a ticking clock, a revelation of where our inhumanity will lead us unless imagination can turn it aside and redirect it, is the total death machine we and our Soviet counterparts have installed in our midst, a crude and brutal embodiment of our blind hatreds as well as of our unreasoning fears. There will be no ritual opening of bodies to affirm our beliefs in the hot center of the total-death machine's maelstrom. There will be only meaningless slaughter and the earth a cold grave.

It requires a special kind of body to prepare such destruction. The sociologist Murray Davis, examining it in the context of human sexuality, characterizes it as Jehovanist. "To condemn sex as much as they do," Davis writes, " . . . Jehovanists must believe that ideally each human being has a self that is highly structured, sharply bounded, unique, integrated, pure, and separated from the selves of others completely and permanently. They dread that this delicate identity will be easily punctured during copulation."[19]

"Jehovanists are better able to tolerate violence than sex," Davis continues, "because violence does less damage to their highly inte-grated . . . conception of the self. By widening the psychic interval between individuals, centrifugal violence sharpens individual selves. But by narrowing the psychic interval between individuals, centripetal sex defuses individual selves. Since self-integrity is more basic to their view of the world than even bodily existence, Jehovanists fear the ability of sex to disintegrate the self far more than the ability of violence to destroy the body. Thus they are far more likely to censor sex . . . than violence, for what is one human life—or even a few million— when a world view is at stake?"[20]

The German scholar Klaus Theweleit ingeniously discovers the Jehovanist view at its most extreme in the diaries, novels, and memoirs of the Freikorps vigilantes of Weimar Germany, fascists who battled in the streets of Munich and by assassination against what they conceived to be a Red Menace and who later formed the core of the Nazi move- ment and counted among its leaders.[21] "Soldier males," Theweleit calls these self-appointed executioners, and finds them horrified by images of floods and bodies. Fears of bodily dissolution obsessed them; they assigned the threat of such potential dissolution to the working-class movements of communism and socialism, which seemed to them to violate traditional political and economic boundaries. Even representa- tive democracy disgusted the Freikorps vigilantes; they considered it government by rabble, "a tenacious bourgeoisie," as one of them wrote, "immersing everything in its slime."[22]

"The crucial point here," Theweleit summarizes, "is that for the soldier male, the flood set loose by the rebels was connected, in some frightening, intolerable way, with his own pent-up streams (which . . . he could perceive only as negativized things, threatening him with dissolution). He could hardly remain indifferent to what those people were doing out there, because the flood, if it came, would burst his boundaries. It wasn't so much his economic position he was defending as his psychic constitution—and in that sense, his very survival."[23] ". . . Not a single drop [could] be allowed to seep through the shell of the body. One little drop of pleasure—a single minute flyspeck on the wall of a house, or a single escapee from a concentration camp— [threatened] to undermine the whole system."[24]

Here we approach the rigid, brittle body of totalitarianism. Jean-Paul Sartre characterizes it perspicaciously in an attack on anti-Semitism: "There are people," Sartre writes, "who are attracted by the permanence of stone. They would like to be solid and impenetrable, they do not want change: for who knows what change might bring? . . . It is as if their own existence were perpetually in suspense. But they want to exist in all ways at once, and all in one instant. They have no wish to acquire ideas, they want them to be innate . . . . They want to adopt a mode of life in which reasoning and the quest for truth play only a subordinate part, in which nothing is sought except what has already been found, in which one never becomes anything else but what one already was."[25]

But Sartre's "diatribe," counters the anthropologist Mary Douglas, "implies a division between ours and the rigid black and white thinking of the anti-Semite. Whereas, of course," writes Douglas, "the yearning for rigidity is in us all. It is part of our human condition to long for hard lines and clear concepts. When we have them we have to either face the fact that some realities elude them, or else blind ourselves to the inadequacy of the concepts."[26]

Which brings the wheel full circle, because to blind ourselves to the inadequacy of our concepts is at some level of awareness to introduce doubt, and to introduce doubt is to invite the destructive wounding that grounds uncertain belief in the body in order to certify it. The monuments in our public parks to the men who died in our wars recall us to our values, but casting them in bronze and removing all traces of their wounding does not return them to life. Better the names carved into the blank wall of the Vietnam war memorial, the individual, identifiable names of the dead not dissolved into abstraction. "I was always embarrassed," Ernest Hemingway wrote of an earlier war, "by the words sacred, glorious, and sacrifice and the expression in vain.

We had heard them, sometimes standing in the rain almost out of earshot, so that only the shouted words came through, and had read them, on proclamations that were slapped up by billposters over other proclamations, now for a long time, and I had seen nothing sacred, and the things that were glorious had no glory and the sacrifices were like the stockyards at Chicago if nothing was done with the meat except to bury it. There were many words that you could not stand to hear and finally only the names of places had dignity. Certain numbers were the same way and certain dates and these with the names of the places were all you could say and have them mean anything."[27] Freud thought that we are all neurotic, and no doubt we are; but certainly on the evidence of the twentieth century we are all infected with the totalitarian. Purity, Mary Douglas argues, is "the enemy of change, of ambiguity and compromise."[28] To some degree we all prefer our religious, national, political, and so-called racial purity to the changing, ambiguous, compromising complexities of diversity, and we are able and too often willing to enforce our purity on others with violence technologically amplified.

In the midst of this confusion, imagination continues modestly and I think bravely to pursue its program of gradually removing prejudice, of opening up and animating the world. In that honest work, the arts—books today, music or painting or dance or theater another day—have an honorable place. They do not generate friendly, mass-producible objects as craft and technology do—chairs that alleviate gravity, vaccines that block disease. Works of art remain only partly realized, arrested in passage between the imaginary and the material world, like the figures caught in mid-passage traversing the plane of the great bronze doors of Renaissance churches, like the digital encoding of a sound sequence or a genome that must be reconstituted to be expressed. Works of art require playback, in the mind or under the proscenium, and in that sense are prodigal of energy and not fully disembodied.

But in a more profound sense they are efficient, because all without exception are programs that generate alternative worlds—utopias, quotidians or anti-utopias, paradises or purgatories or hells. Entering these alternative worlds, we are freed to experience and to measure alternative futures—or presents, or pasts. Readers feel intensely what they read, and incorporate it, imagination calling forth further imagining in millions of men and women and children whose lives otherwise may be severely restricted. They can risk doing so, can examine alternatives, can discover their common humanity and consider change and even revolution, because doubt within the pages of a book does not culminate in wounding, because death has no dominion, because ripe fruit never falls. If phenomena are inexhaustible generators of meaning, if phenomena contain their own ground and dictate how we understand them, if the lived body is the bearer of meaning,[29] it is also true that works of art, half in and half out of imagination, half in and half out of the body, half in and half out of the world, partake to a greater or lesser degree of the nature of phenomena, are literally as well as figuratively phenomenal. We understand that of them. We understand that they are one of a kind, as any human being is one of a kind, and cherish them proportionately. It is because they are not quite real that they are potentially immortal.

If the total-death machine is a minotaur, now at the end of this bloodiest of centuries we approach the center of its maze. Imagination is Ariadne's thread, unraveled to lead us out. The function of creativity, the great human project, is the alleviation of pain. By all means let's get on with it.

Richard Rhodes

NOTES

1. Elaine Scarry, *The Body in Pain: The Making and Unmaking of the World* (New York: Oxford University Press, 1985), p. 285(Scarry's emphasis). The argument in Scarry's book is basic to this essay.

2. Michael Polanyi, *The Tacit Dimension* (Garden City, N.Y.: Doubleday, 1966), p. 4.

3. Paraphrased from Polanyi, ibid., p. 29.

4. Cf. Kenneth Joel Shapiro, *Bodily Reflective Modes* (Durham, N. C.: Duke University Press, 1985), pp. 101-3. Shapiro's schema in this instance comes from Piaget.

5. Polanyi, *Tacit Dimension*, p. xi.

6. Alice Kimball Smith and Charles Weiner, *Robert Oppenheimer: Letters and Recollections* (Cambridge: Harvard University Press, 1980), pp. 315 ff.

7. Scarry, *The Body*, p. 306.

8. Niels Bohr, *Atomic Physics and Human Knowledge* (New York: John Wiley, 1958), p. 31.

9. Scarry, *The Body*, p. 128 (with emphasis deleted).

10. Cf. Hans Kruuk, "The Urge to Kill," *New Scientist*, 28 June 1972.

11. Quoted in Richard Rhodes, *The Making of the Atomic Bomb* (New York: Simon & Schuster, 1986), p. 615.

12. For a discussion of these numbers, cf. Gil Elliot, *Twentieth Century Book of the Dead* (New York: C. Scribner, 1972), pp. 211 ff.

13. Ruth Leger Sivard, *World Military and Social Expenditures 1987-88*, 12th ed. (Leesburg, Va.: World Priorities, 1987).

14. U.S. and Soviet strategic nuclear forces, end of 1987. *Bulletin of the Atomic Scientists* 44 (1988): 56.

15. International Committee of Experts in Medical Sciences and Public Health to Implement Resolution WHA34.38, *Effects of Nuclear War on Health and Health Services* (Geneva: World Health Organization, 1984).

16. Cf. P. J. Crutzen and J. W. Birks, "The Atmosphere after a Nuclear War: Twilight at Noon," *Ambrio* 11 (1982): 114-25; R. P. Turco, O. B. Toon, et al., "Nuclear Winter: Global Consequences of Multiple Nuclear Explosions," *Science* 222 (1983): 1283-92; and National Research Council, *The Effects on the Atmosphere of a Major Nuclear Exchange* (Washington: National Academy Press, 1985).

17. D. S. Greer and L. S. Rifkin, "The Immunological Impact of Nuclear Warfare," in *The Medical Implications of Nuclear War*, ed. F. Solomon and R. Q. Marston (Washington: National Academy Press, 1986).

18. Elliot, *Twentieth Century Book of the Dead*, p. 6.

19. Murray S. Davis, *Smut* (Chicago: University of Chicago Press, 1983), pp. 123 ff.

20. Ibid., p. 196.

21. Cf. Klaus Theweleit, *Male Fantasies*, vol. 1 (Minneapolis: University of Minnesota Press, 1987).

22. Ibid., p. 394.

23. Ibid., p. 427.

24. Ibid., p. 266.

25. Jean-Paul Sartre, *Portrait of an Anti-Semite* (London: Secker & Warburg, 1948). Quoted in Mary Douglas, *Purity and Danger* (New York: Praeger, 1966), p. 162.

26. Douglas, *Purity and Danger,* p. 162.

27. Ernest Hemingway, *A Farewell to Arms* (New York: Collier Books, 1929, 1957), p. 185.

28. Douglas, *Purity and Danger,* p. 162.

29. Paraphrased from Shapiro, *Bodily Reflective Modes*, pp. 41, 81.

T H E   W R I T I N G   L I F E
From Beirut to Jerusalem to Washington

I am not going to talk here specifically about my book, or specifically about journalism, but rather about the craft of reporting and the very different writing-reporting experiences that I have had in my brief career.

I realize that to the casual observer it looks as though I was a journalist who wrote a book. End of story. It has been done a thousand times before and will be done a thousand times more. Actually, though, I have had what I consider to be at least four distinctly different writing-reporting experiences in my career, each of which imparted to me some very important and distinctly different lessons. It is those lessons which will be my subject here.

This lecture is going to weave together a lot of different strands. I break my own writing life into four parts, each of which happens to correspond to different geographical locations in which I have lived as a reporter and writer.

In the beginning there was Beirut—for me at least—then Jerusalem, then writing a book in between Jerusalem and Washington, and finally working as a reporter in Washington.

I think that the most important thing Beirut teaches you, or maybe forces you to learn as a journalist, is how to operate in a city without officials. It is a particularly stark lesson for anyone who comes from

Washington, which is a city in which there are only officials! But in Beirut there are none. There are really no officials who count and no government to speak of. That is why I entitled the chapter in my book about reporting from Beirut: "Beirut, City of Versions." Because, as my colleague the late Bill Farrell once observed, "There is no truth in Beirut, only versions."

I once described to someone what it is like to be a reporter in Beirut. I said it's like you are standing there watching this white light of truth coming at you. But before it hits you it is refracted through this prism of Lebanese factions and fiefs and religious groups, so that before it reaches your eyes it is splayed out in fifteen different directions. And your challenge as a reporter is to grab a little bit of the blue band, and a little bit of the red band, a little bit of the green band, and try to paint as close a picture of reality as you possibly can. It's like being in a dark tunnel, aided only by a single candle looking for the light at the other end. And you see a light and chase it only to discover that it is someone else also with a candle, also looking for the light at the other end.

Now this situation had its advantages and disadvantages. The upside was that what made Beirut such an exciting place to be as a reporter is that you could get to see things there that you would not be able to see in virtually any other reporting environment. There were no police sawhorses in Beirut that separated the reporters from the actors. There was no precinct spokesman who said, "I'm sorry, you can't go down that road, but I'll tell you what's happened." In Beirut, you could get into your car and drive as far as your courage or your gas tank would take you. That meant some reporters not only drove right into the battle but drove through the battle and out the other side. There was literally nothing to stop you. As a result, you got to see scenes, you got to see emotions, you got to see battles at a proximity which you could not imagine on any other story. The only thing I can compare it to is being at a theater in which you could actually go up on stage in the middle of play and talk to the actors while they were reciting their lines.

"So, tell me Hamlet, what's this problem you have with your stepfather?"

For a reporter or writer that is the ultimate high. It really enabled me to enlarge myself as a writer very early in my career by exposing me to an unusually broad range of emotions and bizarre encounters from one end of the human spectrum to the other. Having to, and being able to, describe some of the incredible scenes that cross your path on any given day in Beirut stretches your writing muscles like a literary aerobic.

The downside of that kind of environment though is that because nothing is official everything is official. At some level, everybody's story becomes equally true, everyone's version equally valid. A reporter could get up in the morning, sit down at his typewriter, and write, "15 Christians were massacred on the Green Line today by 30 Shiite Moslems."

Who can check? Are you going to go down to the Green Line and check? I'm not going to go down to the Green Line and check. The police are not going to go down to the Green Line and check. It is an exaggerated example, to be sure, but what I am trying to say is that in a paradoxical way such an environment really teaches you a writer's discipline. As a reporter you really had to go that extra mile yourself to confirm, or try to confirm, what was true and what was false. You did not have the luxury of being able to just pick up the phone and say: "O. K., Mr. Spokesman, what's true and what's not?" You had to report every story ten times and from ten different angles if you wanted to make sure that it was correct. For the best reporters this imposed a great burden. For the worst reporters it really gave them free rein. And that's why we saw some remarkable excesses in reporting from Beirut during the summer of 1982. One reporter for a major American network reported one day that six square blocks of West Beirut were "dust and rubble."

Six square blocks? Do you know how big six square blocks is? I mean there was a lot of dust and a lot of rubble there. But it wasn't six square blocks, except on the Green Line where fighting had been going on for years. But who could check?

What often happened as a result of this freewheeling reporting environment was that because we as reporters are so trained to rely on sources—rely on them sometimes as a crutch, someone who you can call with one dial of the phone who will fill you in authoritatively on the real story—some people almost invented sources or spokesmen where none existed. What I mean by that was there was a wire service in Beirut that wrote a story one day which it attributed to "Leftist sources." According to Leftist sources . . . .

I wondered to myself: "What is a Leftist source? Is that people who are left-handed?" I mean, in West Beirut everyone is a Leftist source. That's like quoting "Jewish sources" in Israel. But people did it in order to get a ring of authenticity into their reporting where none naturally existed.

I think the second thing that Beirut really taught me as a journalist and as a writer was to appreciate the moment. As I noted in my book, some of my colleagues came to Beirut and could not leave because they became hooked on their own adrenaline and on the daily bang-bang that gets you on the front page or the evening news. I was not immune to that myself. But there was always something more for me. When I think back on Beirut now, I barely remember the close calls or the adrenaline highs. Instead, I always come back to certain "moments"— all those remarkable human encounters I got to witness that taught me more about people and what they are made of than the previous twenty-five years of my life. I got to see with my own eyes the boundaries of men's compassion alongside their unfathomable brutality, their ingenuity alongside astounding folly, and their insanity alongside their infinite ability to endure.

Of course for the Lebanese who starred in the moments of my memory, there was no thrill, only the numbing routine of survival, punctuated by an occasional moment of levity. I never forgot that my moments were usually their nightmares. Gerald Butt, the BBC correspondent in Beirut, told me a story that happened toward the end of the summer of '82 that really brought this home to me. A group of Lebanese doctors and nurses had decided to organize a protest march across the Green Line from West Beirut to East Beirut, in order to draw world attention to the Israeli siege, which had caused a shortage of medical supplies in West Beirut. The march took place at the Galerie Sama'an crossing point between East and West, a barren mile-long stretch of road flanked by half-destroyed apartment buildings purged of all life except snipers.

"At the time, I really didn't think about it being dangerous," Butt later recalled. "I just thought, well, here's a story that I should be covering, so I joined the march. There were about 20 doctors and nurses, and someone at the front carried a Red Cross flag. When we got about halfway across the Green Line, I looked around and saw that there was no cover anywhere. We were in the middle of the Green Line! There was shelling nearby, snipers all around, and I was walking with these doctors. I just said to myself, 'What am I doing here?' And then I turned to look back and I saw a Lebanese man just a few meters behind us, and he was leading a white horse. A white horse! It looked like a racehorse . . . . He must have heard that there was going to be a march across the Green Line and he wanted to use us for cover to get his horse out of West Beirut. He probably couldn't feed it because of the shortage of food and water. It was so surreal. These doctors, and the Red Cross flag and the shelling and this man tagging along with his white racehorse."

It is for such moments that a reporter is drawn to Beirut, and stays there long after good sense tells him he should leave. The front-page stories, the six-column headlines over your byline, those were all a great thrill at the time. But they don't last, only the moments do.

Whenever I try to explain this irrational tug of Beirut, I am reminded of that joke that Woody Allen tells at the end of the movie *Annie Hall*. A guy goes to his doctor and says, "Doctor, doctor, I have got a terrible problem, my brother thinks he is a chicken." And the doctor says, "That's crazy, just tell him he's not a chicken." The guy says, "I can't. I need the eggs."

It's the same as a reporter. I kept coming back to Beirut because I needed the eggs. And the eggs were the moments.

An appreciation for those moments which bring a story alive and convey certain universal truths may be the most important lesson any writer could ever learn. You see there is reporting, there is good reporting, and then there is great reporting. What distinguishes one from the other? In my opinion, "good reporting" is a combination of good analysis of an event and good anecdotes—that is, good picturesque moments that really bring the analysis alive. It can be something as simple as the way an official gestured with his hand to something as complicated as a personal family saga. But it is that moment that brings your analysis alive to the reader in a pungent way and in a way in which he or she can really relate to the analytical point you are trying to make. A story that is only anecdotal is like a series of pictures without any text. A story that is only analytical is like a text without any pictures. Now "great reporting" is a combination of great anecdotal moments and great analysis.

For instance, as a reporter in Beirut you could write on any given day that the mood in the city had turned very pessimistic. Or you could try a different approach. My ultimate political source in Beirut was a glassmaker. He was a Lebanese who probably had not even finished high school. He had never heard of George Gallup. But Riyad, as he was called, knew one thing. He knew that when people were ordering glass it meant that they were confident about the future, and confident that a new round of fighting was not about to explode that would shatter their windows. Very simple. When people were upbeat and confident, everyone was replacing windows and business for Riyad boomed. When people felt that the political situation was about to deteriorate or stay bad they replaced their broken windows with plastic sandwich wrap and business for Riyad was awful. He became, like the proverbial Maytag repairman, the loneliest man in town. So you could say to the reader flat out: People in Beirut are pessimistic. Or you could say to the reader that people are pessimistic and now let me tell you about the visit I had last week with my friend Riyad.

This approach requires several things from the writer. First, it means understanding that you constantly need to have your ear to the ground—talking to everyone from presidents to grocers—to have a feel for where the "Story" with a capital *S* is at all times. Second, you constantly have to be on the lookout for the telling anecdote or gesture—and it could come anytime, anywhere—that would illuminate that story. And third, through a process of trial and error, you constantly have to be seeking out these people in whatever country you happen to be living in who are original thinkers. An original thinker is, well, just that—someone who thinks totally for himself, never gets caught up in the conventional wisdom, and has that ability to articulate the universal truths contained in your anecdotes as well as to bring your own analysis to a higher level. That is how I work as a reporter. I am constantly interacting with my environment on one hand, trying to monitor the mood and keep my pulse on where and what the story is, and, at the same time, constantly bringing my anecdotes and intuitions on a platter to the best minds I can find to help me figure out just what they mean.

For instance, there is a story I tell in my book about going to the Bar Mitzvah of an Israeli cousin of mine and being surprised at the fact that he ordered pork chops for lunch at the meal following the ceremony. I just tucked that away and then as soon as I got back to Jerusalem I called one of my original-thinking sources on religious matters, related to him the story, and said: "What does this mean? What does that tell us?" Together my source and I would figure it out like a puzzle. Sometimes these conversations would go on over several days until I, or we, were satisfied that we had gotten to the bottom of it. The best compliment I ever get from a source is when he or she says to me after one of these sessions: "You know, that was fun. I had not really articulated any of these things in this way until you forced me to think about it." I never go to an analytical source looking for "a quote." I always come carrying some problem, scene, encounter, or mystery and ask for help understanding it. I have always found that if you come to these sessions with good questions and good anecdotes, you will take away good insights. Come empty, leave empty—or leave just with "a quote" as opposed to an insight.

The third thing that Beirut taught me as a reporter, paradoxically really, is to appreciate not only the moments, but, just as importantly, the silence. Sometimes a journalist would be kidnapped there and someone would say, "Why him? How could they have kidnapped him? Why, he knew everybody in town."

Well, he may have known everybody who made it their business to have contact with journalists, but that is it. Beirut taught me how little you can really know about a place within which you are living. Take for example February 1984. During that month the Shiites of West Beirut basically mounted a revolution in the streets that took practically everyone in the city by surprise. There was one scene in particular that really drove it home for me. My wife and I were eating lunch at the Commodore Hotel, the clubhouse for all Western journalists. It was one day after the revolt had finished, and this wild-eyed Shiite gunman came into the hotel, stalked through the lobby, and went straight into the bar. The bartender had been expecting him, and had hid all the liquor bottles under the bar and built a pyramid of Pepsi cans where the Johnny Walker once stood. But this Shiite militiaman wasn't fooled. He swept the bartender aside, went behind the bar, and methodically broke every bottle and glass in the house with the butt of his rifle.

The thing I kept thinking about as I watched him was that this guy was probably one of my neighbors. He had been living there all this time, but I didn't know him. My fault, not his. And it really endowed me with a whole new respect for how little I really knew about the subterranean emotions that were coursing under Beirut. In fact, I left Beirut with a variation of Groucho Marx's line that any club that will have me as a member, I don't want to join. Mine was that any official source who will talk to me, I don't want to speak to. Because so often it is the people who talk to journalists who are the ones who never really know what's happening. The people who are out kidnapping journalists, or blowing up marine headquarters, don't give interviews with Time Magazine. They just do it and then come home and quietly savor it over a Turkish coffee. They don't go to the Commodore Hotel bar and sidle up to you and say: "Hey, Friedman, guess what I just blew up!"

I learned to appreciate the silence not only by occasionally getting a glimpse of how vast was the sea of people and actors out there whom

23

I didn't know, but also by occasionally discovering that the real story was in what was not being said, rather than in what was being said.

Take for instance the day the marines' headquarters in Beirut were blown up—October 23, 1983. It was 6:20 A.M. and my wife Ann and I were sleeping in our apartment. We were awakened by an explosion that literally wiggled our whole apartment house, despite the fact that the blast was actually ten miles away. At first I thought it was an earthquake. Ann and I scrambled down the stairs and into our car to see what it was. As we drove out of our neighborhood, though, the thing I remembered most was that there was a small group of Lebanese men playing tennis at the local clay court club. I mean, here 241 Americans had just been blown up, and they were playing tennis. They didn't know where the explosion had happened, of course. But the ground, the court, the very clay under their feet, must have shaken them to the core. And later in the day, when everyone knew what had happened, people were still playing tennis. That really became an enormous statement for me about their real attitudes toward the Americans in Lebanon. They loved the marines when they came, supposedly to protect the Lebanese from anarchy. But when the Lebanese discovered that the marines could not even protect themselves, people came to look upon them with disdain. Now I could have gone around to hundreds of people and interviewed them and sooner or later that sentiment would have been expressed. Or, I could do what I did in this case—just listen to their silence.

The last thing Beirut really taught me, maybe as a derivation of this last point, was a tremendous respect for the street and the wisdom of the street. One of the things that is great about working in a city with no officials is that you learn to depend on your grocer, your maid, and your local butcher as your political sources. Because when no one is the government, everyone is the government. When no one is an official source, everyone is an official source. The way I would go about writing a story in Beirut, nine times out of ten times, was not to seek out someone in the Lebanese government, be it what it may, and not to seek some "Western diplomat" or unnamed official. Rather, I would literally sit down, draw up a list of all the nurses, grocers, and bankers I knew— all the people who interacted with society at large—and then go talk to them one by one. My best sources in Beirut, I always used to say, were bankers. Because bankers become psychoanalysts in their own way by observing what people do with their most valued assets. But I would also interview nurses often, and grocery store owners, and yes, even proverbial taxi drivers. Once I had a sense of what the street felt like, what the street was saying, I had a sense of the limits of politics. It didn't matter what President Amine Gemayel declared was going on, or what he was intending to do or not do. I knew exactly what would fly or not fly politically from what the street was telling me.

I'll never forget, one day I was having lunch with Elie Salem, Lebanon's foreign minister in the early 1980s. It was a fancy lunch in East Beirut, with twelve senior foreign correspondents in attendance. Well, he was going on and on, telling us about the political situation, how everything was going to improve, how Lebanon really was not locked in civil war and, for all that I remember, how the moon was made of green cheese. Anyway, I was seated directly across from him, and at one point I started asking him about what he thought were the political implications of the mood in the street. Moslem West Beirut was under curfew at the time and Christian East Beirut, where Salem lived, wasn't. And if you lived in West Beirut, as I did, you could feel the anger there just welling up in the streets. Eventually I said to Salem, "Mr. Minister, do you know what's going on in the street? Do you realize the pressures people feel?" And then I described to him what my maid and grocer had all been saying to me.

I don't remember what he answered, but what always stuck in my mind was that before he did he turned to his secretary, who was seated at the far end of the table, and he said to her in Arabic, "I guess you were right." And then he turned and answered me. In other words, it was clear that his secretary had been telling him just what I had said—as he got in and out of his limousine, in and out of his bubble. And he must have been dismissing it. But it took me, someone from outside his bubble, to really confirm what this woman of the street was telling him.

Moving to reporting from Jerusalem, what did I learn about writing there? In many ways it was a totally different assignment for me compared to Beirut. The first thing I learned in Jerusalem, or had to come to terms with, was the whole question of objectivity, and what exactly does it mean for a writer to be "objective."

It wasn't an accident that it was in Jerusalem where I felt this question most acutely, because I was the first Jewish reporter the New York Times ever assigned to Jerusalem full time. The Times had for many years had an unwritten rule that said you don't send a Jew to Israel because people will say that he or she is not objective—can't possibly be objective—no matter how or what they write.

So I had to think out in my own mind: "What does being objective as a journalist really mean?" What would I answer if someone came up to me and said: "You are Jewish, you are emotionally involved. You can't by definition be objective."

If you look at most definitions of objectivity in journalism text-books or elsewhere, they will basically, in my opinion, equate objectiv-ity with ignorance. In other words, they will advise that if you want to get the most objective journalist possible for the Middle East find a

Gentile from Wyoming who has never met an Arab or Jew in his life and he or she will be perfect. Now, to that I say, nonsense. Objectivity should not be synonymous with ignorance.

Objectivity in my mind is a tension—a tension between two conflicting impulses: understanding and disinterest. What do I mean by that? I can't possibly write a fair story, an insightful story, an honest story about any one of my readers unless I get close enough to you to understand what you are really about, unless I gain knowledge of, or acquire the background into, what makes you tick. I can't possibly write a fair story about Israelis or Palestinians unless I become knowledgeable about their history, and also get close enough to them as individuals so that I am almost inside their heads, looking at the world as they do. Because without that kind of deep understanding—understanding that borders on sympathy—I can't possibly be fair.

But at the same time, I have to maintain a certain distance and level of disinterest, because if I don't, I will understand only them, and that cannot possibly produce objective reporting either. That is why I insist that objectivity is a constant tension between understanding and disinterest. And you are never going to get it perfectly balanced in every story or every book. Sometimes you may be a little too distant; sometimes you may be a little too understanding. But you've got to feel that tension inside you all the time. Understanding without disinterest lapses into commitment. And disinterest without understanding lapses into banality. So whenever anyone asked me how I as a Jew could be "objective," my answer was always that objectivity is not something you are born with, it is not something that you can claim on the basis of your biography, it is a state of mind that you have to aspire to and anyone—Christian, Moslem, or Jew—can aspire to it. Judge me on what I write, not on my birth certificate.

Another thing that Jerusalem really teaches you, in a funny way, is a real appreciation for words and exactitude. I always say that Jerusalem is the only assignment where they will kill a reporter for a conjunction. As a New York Times reporter in particular, you have to work there under a tremendous spotlight. It is like no other reporting assignment when it comes to the degree to which your copy is scrutinized and psychoanalyzed by readers. "Why did you put a 'but' there and not a comma? Why did you put a comma there and not a semicolon? What does that say about you? What does that say about your mother or your attitude toward Judaism?" These are all questions that were hurled at me at one time or another, and they taught me to weigh my words very carefully.

I happened to arrive in Jerusalem around the time that the first national unity government was being formed in September 1984, but I was off on vacation the day the new cabinet was actually announced. So my Israeli assistant, Moshe Brilliant, who was in his early seventies, ended up reporting and filing the story. The cabinet announcement happened to break late at night so Moshe had to dictate the story to the New York Times over a scratchy phone line. He also had to dictate the cabinet list. Speaking into the phone he began at the top and went right down: "Prime Minister, from the Labor Party, Shimon Peres; Vice Prime Minister and Foreign Minister, from the Likud Party, Yitzhak Shamir." Well, when he got to Dr. Joseph Burg, a very learned Orthodox politician, he said: "Dr. Joseph Burg, veteran National Religious Party leader, Minister of Religious Affairs." Well, the person on the other end of the phone heard, "Bedouin National Religious Party leader," not veteran. So, the New York Times comes out at 11:00 P.M., the cabinet list is there, and it says Joseph Burg, Bedouin National Religious Party Leader. It is hard to imagine a bigger mistake. No sooner was the paper out than someone called Dr. Burg in Israel and someone from Israel called the New York Times and, I'm told, the story was corrected in real time before the next edition.

As much as I thought that I had learned every lesson I possibly could as a writer in Jerusalem, to weigh my words very, very carefully, and think about every comma and conjunction, lo and behold I wrote my book and I discovered I hadn't learned anything at all—judging from some of the reactions. It amazes me that with all the experience I had as a reporter I could write a book that would produce reactions that I totally didn't anticipate. And that it could produce reactions that were so widely divergent. It has fascinated me to see the degree to which, with a book as opposed to a newspaper story, people take away from it what they bring to it.

I get about a dozen letters a week on my book from people who have read it. One will call me a "self-hating Jew" and the next will praise my book as a compelling saga and talk of "fervent appreciation." Same book, same mailbag, same day. Both letters from Jews. And I am not quite sure what to do about it. I thought about, for the paper-back, tinkering with things. Maybe I wasn't clear enough and should add a paragraph here, or delete something there. But I eventually realized that this book has become a sort of out-of-body experience. I wrote it and now it's out there, and it seems to have taken on a life and persona all its own. And it's almost no longer mine in a way. That's both humbling and frustrating.

Finally let me make a few observations about writing from Washington. The transition from Beirut to Jerusalem to book to Washington is a strange one indeed, particularly the leap from foreign reporting in the Middle East to diplomatic reporting in Washington. What I always tell people is that I feel as though I have gone from covering a street to covering a hall, and from covering a drama unfolding before my eyes to covering a policy that is invisible. You can't say, "I met the policy today. She wept on my shoulder," or " I saw the policy bleeding today at the C-Street entrance to the State Department."

When people ask me what I do for a living, I like to tell them that I cover people who watch CNN. Not only am I not there, but they are not there either. And so I have gone from being able to smell the street in my own nostrils to being three steps removed, and that can be enormously frustrating for a writer who depends on anecdote and texture to bring his analysis alive. It kills me when I meet people in Washington who will say to me, "Oh, I loved your reporting from Jerusalem." And then they will say, "What are you doing now?" People just don't remember stories based on "Administration sources said today."

Another frustration I find about working in Washington, particularly as the diplomatic correspondent, is that your world shrinks to twelve people. You see, when I was in Jerusalem or Beirut and some government spokesman would say, "Well, it's not like that in Gaza or Sidon." I could just answer back, "Yeh, well I was just in Gaza and let me tell you what it is like." I would go for months in both cities without talking to anyone resembling an official. You can't do that in Washington, because here there are only officials. And here, it doesn't really matter what you may think reality is out there. What matters is how the top officials in the government see it, since they are the ones creating the policy and it is the invisible policy that we cover. As a reporter you always have to walk that tightrope between maintaining access to the twelve or so officials who really know what is going on and, at the same time, not getting so close to them that you can't stand back and kick them in the shins when you have to.

I am still trying to figure out how you bring Washington alive.

How do you bring an arms control story alive? One of the things that I have tried to bring to my reporting in Washington, which is almost impossible, is a continued appreciation or healthy respect for the street and for the wild earth. Because when you look at the world from here, it's like what a friend of mine calls: "Watching tennis played on a vertical court." Now, tennis is usually played on a horizontal court. But you come here and people start talking about the "Middle East peace process," and about how Shamir is going to accept this plan and Arafat that plan. And all I can do is sit back and say to myself, "Yes, but what about my grocer in Jerusalem? What will he accept?" What about the wild earth? The first thing that happens to you when you come to Washington is you lose touch with that wild earth. And when you lose touch with the wild earth you are always going to be surprised by something, whether you are an official or a journalist or an author.

Thomas L. Friedman

ACKNOWLEDGMENTS

The Board of Directors of the National Book Foundation gratefully
acknowledges the support of the following donors for National Book
Week 1990: Arcata Graphics, Association of American Publishers,
Book-of-the-Month Club, Consolidated Edison Company of New
York, Inc., Exxon Corporation, Harper & Row, Niagara Trust, S. A.,
Random House, Inc./ S. I. Newhouse Foundation, and Women's
Media Group.

C O L O P H O N

Type
Helvetica, Helvetica Narrow, and Times

Composition
Created electronically using Aldus Pagemaker®
on the Apple® Macintosh® computer by GFC

Cover Paper
Mohawk Superfine Softwhite Regular Finish 80#

Text Paper
Mohawk Superfine Softwhite Eggshell Finish 80#

Printing
Professional Printing Services, Inc.
Glen Allen, Virginia

Illustration
John Crank and Bob Riggs as derived
from Leonardo Da Vinci's canon of proportions

Design
Geary, Flynn & Crank, Inc.
Richmond, Virginia